Kansas City Cooks
For Harvesters

D1451115

HARVESTERS
COMMUNITY FOOD NETWORK

Harvesters' Mission

We help people in need by:

Collecting food and household products from
community and industry sources;

Distributing these products and providing
nutrition services through a network of
nonprofit agencies;

Offering leadership and education programs to
increase community awareness of hunger, and
to generate solutions to end hunger.

Forks & Corks

presents

Kansas City Cooks
For Harvesters

Kansas City's Best Restaurants

Share Their Recipes

Copyright© 2004 Harvesters - The Community Food Network

Cover Illustration Copyright © 2003 Ann Willoughby

Cover Illustration: Ann Willoughby
Cover and Book Design: Willoughby Design Group

Cookbook Development Committee:
Dee Barwick, Pati Chasnoff, Tina Hoover, Bob Merrigan,
Michelle Pierceall, Melanie Thompson

Production: Options Publishing
Recipe Production: JoAnne Owens
                    Teresa Sosinski

All rights reserved. No portion of this book may be reproduced—
mechanically, electronically, or by any other means,
including photocopying—without written permission.

ISBN 1-878686-29-1

Printed in the U.S.A.

First printing October 2004

Harvesters - The Community Food Network
3801 Topping Avenue
Kansas City, MO 64129

Table of Contents

The challenge of hunger in mid-America is not centered in scarcity, but in distribution. The solution lies in getting the food to where it is needed most. As Kansas City's only food bank, Harvesters has become the community's link between an abundant food supply and people in need.

When founders organized in 1979, they were responding to a disturbing social concern: hunger in our community. Since then, Harvesters has become an essential partner with over 550 charitable agencies. These agencies include emergency food pantries, soup kitchens, shelters, day care centers and senior centers. Together we feed the weakest and most vulnerable members of our community – the sick, the elderly, and the very young. In fact, Harvesters serves more than 160,000 different people each year, with almost half being children and elderly.

The need in our community is represented by tens of thousands of men, women and children who are hungry or at risk of hunger. They are people like the elderly couple you may know who retired with a modest, yet adequate income until the sudden expense of caring for grandchildren or dealing with medical issues rendered their finances insufficient. Or maybe they are the single parent or the young couple working low-wage jobs and inwardly dreading the havoc that one financial set-back will wreak on their fragile budget. Put yourself in the place of the professional who has lost a job and is having difficulty finding a comparable position in a difficult economy, and you will experience the same insecurities faced by the people Harvesters serves.

Harvesters' mission doesn't end with the collection and distribution of food. We believe that a long-term solution to hunger involves leadership and outreach programs which educate and increase awareness. Our outreach programs teach children and adults the importance of good nutrition and how to prepare balanced meals inexpensively.

Without community support, however, our mission is not achievable. We exist solely because the community enables us to. You can make a difference by joining us in the fight against hunger.

Karen Haren, Executive Director

Forks & Corks

From its beginnings, Forks & Corks has been an event largely inspired– and enabled – by the generosity of the restaurant and beverage community.

In 1989, one of the city's leading restaurateurs, Steve Cole of Café Allegro, helped bring a food and wine tasting event known nationally as "Taste of the Nation" to Kansas City. For eight years, Cole championed the event and raised hundreds of thousands of dollars to fight hunger . . . locally, through Harvesters and, more broadly, through the national sponsor organization, Share Our Strength.

In 1996, concerned about the growing need for hunger relief in this area, local organizers created "Forks & Corks" a food and wine tasting event which would be dedicated solely to fighting hunger in Kansas City.

Since its inception, Forks & Corks has become one of the most widely recognized – and respected – charitable events in the city. Each year, more than 50 of Kansas City's finest restaurants and beverage purveyors host some 1,500 caring and committed residents who sample and savor the city's most celebrated fare.

At the same time Forks & Corks was created, organizers began planning Chefs Classic . . . an exclusive, sophisticated evening featuring a carefully planned gourmet meal accompanied by specially selected premier wines. Initially, this event was launched to help cover Forks & Corks expenses, but each event has become highly successful in its own right. Held annually at the American Restaurant, Chefs Classic hosts many of nation's finest chefs for a one-of-a-kind dining experience.

Most recently, volunteers have developed another related benefit known as Iron Fork. Based loosely on the Food Network's Iron Chef, Iron Fork is an upbeat, contemporary event that combines a light-hearted competition between local chefs with "samplings" from select local restaurants.

The success of Forks & Corks – and its related events – is a tribute to the commitment of a community . . . but especially the dedication of the restaurants and beverage purveyors who so graciously dedicate their time and resources to fight hunger in Kansas City. At a time when so much is asked of so many, Kansas City's food service community continues to join together to help thousands of Kansas City's hungry through Harvesters.

The recipes that follow are a celebration of the skill, talent and selflessness of our local chefs and restaurants. We hope you enjoy preparing them.

, Event Chairman

9

FOOD RESCUE

Good food shouldn't go to waste. Through
Harvesters' Food Rescue program, prepared excess
food is picked up from restaurants, corporate
cafeterias and hospitals, and delivered to on-site
feeding programs such as soup kitchens, homeless
shelters, domestic abuse shelters, senior centers
and child care centers. The non-profit agencies
that receive the prepared food have come to rely
on it to augment the hot meals they provide to the
children, adults and elderly people they serve.

...to begin

CRAB CAKES WITH CHILI LIME SAUCE
EBT Restaurant

Sauce
1 cup mayonnaise
1 tablespoon chili powder
1 teaspoon chopped garlic
Juice of 1 lime
Pinch of salt
Pinch of white pepper

Crab Cakes
1 pound crab meat
2 cups breadcrumbs, divided
1 egg
1/2 cup Worcestershire sauce
1 tablespoon Dijon mustard
1 tablespoon chopped chives
1 teaspoon chopped garlic
1 teaspoon hot pepper sauce
Juice of 1 lemon
Salt and black pepper to taste
1/2 cup butter

For the chili lime sauce, in a small bowl combine all ingredients. Cover and refrigerate for at least one hour before serving.

For the crab cakes, in a large bowl combine crab, 1 cup breadcrumbs, egg, Worcestershire sauce, mustard, chives, garlic, hot pepper sauce and lemon juice. Add salt and pepper to taste, mixing lightly. Form mixture into balls, using a generous half cup for each. Roll in the remaining breadcrumbs and form into patty shape. In a sauté pan melt butter over medium-high heat. Cook cakes until golden brown, about 3 minutes for each side. Serve with chili lime sauce.

Makes 8 to 10 patties.

CHEF'S NOTE
This recipe has been on the EBT menu since the restaurant opened in 1974.

BROILED SEA SCALLOPS WRAPPED IN BACON
WITH APRICOT CHUTNEY
Morton's, The Steakhouse – Kansas City

Apricot Chutney
1/2 cup apricot marmalade
1/4 cup horseradish, strained
2 teaspoons freshly
   cracked black pepper

Scallops
12 slices bacon
12 large sea scallops
   (1 to 1 1/2 ounces each)
2 tablespoons melted butter
8 large leaves spinach,
   washed and stems removed
2 lemons, halved

For the chutney, in a small bowl smooth marmalade with whisk. Add horseradish and pepper. Blend thoroughly and refrigerate until thoroughly chilled.

For the scallops, place bacon on a wire rack in a 350-degree oven. Cook until half done, approximately 14 minutes. Remove from oven and wrap each scallop with a bacon strip. Slide scallops onto bamboo skewers, 3 scallops per skewer, leaving a 1-inch gap between each scallop. Place skewers in a buttered pie tin. Brush scallops lightly with melted butter. Place under broiler for 8 minutes, turning once. To serve, place 2 spinach leaves in center of each plate. Top one with 2 tablespoons of apricot chutney and a lemon half. Place 3 scallops on top of the other spinach leaf.

Makes 4 servings.

CRISPY COCONUT SHRIMP
Isle of Capri - Farraddays

16 jumbo shrimp, peeled,
    deveined and butterflied,
    tails intact
1 cup flour
1 cup buttermilk
1 1/2 cups shredded coconut
3 to 5 cups peanut or vegetable oil
2 lemons, halved, for garnish
4 leaves radicchio, for garnish
Parsley, for garnish

Dip each shrimp first in the flour, then in the buttermilk and then the coconut, pressing coconut into shrimp. Deep fat fry at 340 degrees until golden brown, about 1 minute. Drain shrimp on paper towels and garnish with lemon, radicchio and parsley. Makes 4 servings.

Makes 4 servings.

CHEF'S NOTE
Serve with fruit skewer made of pineapple, strawberry and orange and sprinkled with coconut.

PEAR, ARUGULA, GRUYERE PIZZA ON PASTA CRUST
Feasts of Fancy Catering

Pasta Crust
1 cup finely ground semolina flour
1 cup all-purpose flour
1/2 teaspoon salt
2 eggs
1 egg yolk
2 tablespoons water, if needed

Topping
Olive oil
4 cups shredded Gruyere cheese
3 pears, cored and sliced
2 cups thin strips of arugula which
   has been washed and
   thoroughly dried
Salt and pepper to taste

For the pasta dough, in the bowl of a mixer combine both flours and salt. Add eggs and egg yolk and mix on medium speed with the dough hook until dough comes together to form a ball. If needed, add water a small amount at a time until dough comes together. Chill dough for one hour. When ready to bake, preheat oven to 350 degrees. Divide dough into four pieces. On a lightly floured surface roll each piece out to 1/8-inch thickness. If using a pasta machine, roll each piece out to #4 thickness. Brush dough lightly with olive oil and bake 10 to 12 minutes until barely crisp. Let cool slightly.

To assemble pizza, brush cooled crust lightly with olive oil. Begin layering the topping ingredients on each of the crusts, starting with half of the cheese, then the pear slices, following with the remaining cheese and finishing with the arugula. Sprinkle pizzas with salt and pepper and bake at 350 degrees until cheese is melted.

Makes 4 pizzas.

CRESPELLE
La Bodega

Crepes
2 eggs
1 pint half & half
1 1/2 cups all-purpose flour
1/2 teaspoon salt
2 tablespoons vegetable oil

Crespelle Mix
1 tablespoon olive oil
2 bunches green onions, diced
1 (8-ounce) package cream cheese
8 ounces feta cheese
1/4 cup fresh basil, chopped
18 roma tomatoes, seeded and
   cut into 1/2-inch pieces
Salt and pepper to taste

For the crepes, in a mixing bowl combine eggs and half & half. Add the flour, salt and oil. Mix until well combined. Heat an 8-inch skillet over medium high heat until skillet is hot. Pour about 1/4 cup of the batter into the skillet. Tilt the pan and swirl quickly until the batter covers the bottom. Cook the crepe for 1 to 2 minutes or until it is golden brown. Loosen the edge of the crepe, turn and brown the other side lightly. Transfer the crepe to a plate. Make crepes with remaining batter in the same manner until you have 7 or 8 crepes. Stack crepes in between sheets of waxed paper.

For the crespelle mix, in a small skillet heat olive oil over medium heat and sauté green onions for 2 to 3 minutes. In a medium bowl combine cream cheese and feta cheese. Add green onions, basil, tomatoes and salt and pepper to taste. Mix well.

Preheat oven to 350 degrees. To assemble crespelle, in the 8-inch skillet place three of the crepes so that they overlap in the center and hang over the outer edge. Spoon about 1 1/2 cups of the crespelle mix into the center and level it out, packing down lightly. Lay one crepe over the mix and pack down lightly. Repeat layers of mix and crepes, packing down lightly between layers, until mix is gone; ending with a crepe. Fold the three overhanging edges of the crepes toward the center to hold crespelle together. Turn upside down onto a cutting board and cut into six to eight wedges. Place the wedges on a cookie sheet and bake for 10 to 15 minutes or until filling is hot and edges are crisp but pieces are soft to the touch.

Makes 6 to 8 servings.

Wine Suggestion: Remondo Palacios La Placet

FRICO CON PATATE E CIPOLLA

Montasio Cheese Crisp with Potatoes and Onions

Lidia Bastianich – Lidia's Kansas City

2 medium-large baking potatoes
2 tablespoons olive oil
1 cup sliced onions
3/4 pound montasio cheese,
   rind removed, shredded
Salt and pepper to taste

**Wine Suggestion:
Caldaro Pinot
Bianco**

In a saucepan with enough water to cover boil the potatoes in their skins for 25 to 30 minutes, keeping them on the firm side. Remove from heat and drain off water. When potatoes are cool enough to handle, but still warm, peel and slice them 1/4 inch thick. In a skillet heat the olive oil and sauté the onions until wilted. Add potatoes and cook until golden. Add salt and pepper to taste. In a 6-inch skillet over medium heat sprinkle 1/4 of the cheese evenly to cover the pan, top with half of the potato mixture and spread evenly. Sprinkle another 1/4 of the cheese to cover the potato mixture. Let the cheese at the bottom form a crust (approximately 8 to 10 minutes), flip over with the spatula and let the other side become crisp. Remove the frico from the skillet and repeat process to make a second frico. Cut fricos in quarters to serve.

Makes 4 servings.

CHEDDAR CHUTNEY CHEESECAKE
The Catering Company

4 1/2 (8-ounce) packages
   cream cheese, softened
3 eggs
1/3 cup grated onion
3/4 teaspoon cayenne
1 1/4 cups grated sharp
   cheddar cheese
3/4 teaspoon sherry
1/2 cup chopped pecans
1 cup mango chutney, divided
1/2 cup pecan halves, for garnish

Preheat oven to 350 degrees. Prepare an 8-inch spring form pan by lining bottom and sides completely with foil, and allowing foil to extend above the sides of the pan. Coat foil with cooking spray. Using an electric mixer, combine cream cheese, eggs, onion, cayenne, cheese, sherry, chopped pecans and 1/2 cup chutney. Beat until just blended and smooth. Pack into the spring form pan. Swirl the remaining chutney and pecan halves over the top. Place the pan into a baking dish and fill half way with warm water. Bake for 1 hour or until a knife inserted in center comes out clean. Cool on rack for 30 minutes and remove sides of pan. Cool for 3 hours or overnight before serving.

Makes 15 to 20 servings.

ONION PUFFS
The Catering Company

12 to 15 slices white
    sandwich bread
1 cup mayonnaise
1 1/2 cups freshly grated
    parmesan cheese
2 tablespoons grated onion
2 tablespoons chopped green
    onion tops
Freshly cracked black
    pepper to taste

Using a 1-inch cookie cutter cut out bread rounds and place on a baking sheet. Place in a 200-degree oven until completely dry, about 15 to 20 minutes. Meanwhile, in a mixing bowl combine mayonnaise, parmesan cheese, onion, green onion and pepper. Spread mixture on dried rounds and place under broiler until golden and bubbly, or two to three minutes. Let cool for a minute or two and serve.

Makes about 50 pieces.

CHEF'S NOTE
Grate onion over a paper towel, which will absorb the moisture. It's best to use an old-fashioned grater, not food processor.

The 1-inch cookie cutters, sometimes called hors d'oeuvre cutters, can be found at specialty food shops.

GOAT CHEESE FLANS
40 Sardines

4 ounces soft goat cheese
2 large eggs
1/3 cup heavy whipping cream
Salt and pepper to taste

CHEF'S NOTE

Serve with crisp crackers and grilled hearty breads.

Many garnishes will complement the flans: marinated mushrooms, slow-roasted summer tomatoes, asparagus with toasted garlic cloves and olive oil. And of course, any light, refreshing salad.

Preheat oven to 325 degrees. Butter eight 2-ounce molds. In a large bowl place the cheese and slowly mix in the eggs. Blend by hand until mixture is very smooth. Slowly add cream and mix until well blended. Season with salt and pepper. Pour batter into molds and place in a large baking dish which has been filled half way with warm water. Bake for 25 to 30 minutes or until set. When flans are completely cool, unmold by turning upside down on plates and tapping lightly.

Makes 8 servings.

CHANTERELLE AND CHEVRE PIE
City Tavern

Crust

1 cup all-purpose flour

1/4 teaspoon salt

1/2 teaspoon black pepper

1/2 cup shortening

1/4 cup cold water

Filling

1 tablespoon butter

4 tablespoons finely chopped
fresh garlic, divided

1/2 pound chanterelle mushrooms,
cleaned and trimmed (can
substitute porcini or shiitake
mushrooms)

1 pound chevre (goat cheese)

2 tablespoons finely chopped
fresh thyme

Salt and freshly ground
black pepper to taste

CHEF'S NOTE
*Serve with dressed
greens or as an
accompaniment to your
favorite fall main dish.*

Preheat oven to 350 degrees. For the crust, in a small bowl combine flour, salt and pepper. Add shortening. Cut shortening into flour mixture until pea-size balls form. Add water slowly, until all flour is moistened. Form dough into a ball. On a lightly floured surface, roll dough into a 12-inch circle, transfer to a 9-inch pie plate. Trim to about 1/2 inch beyond edge. Fold extra pastry under and crimp. Set aside.

For the filling, in a skillet melt the butter over medium heat. Add 2 tablespoons garlic and cook for about 2 minutes, just until soft. Stir in mushrooms, then sauté until slightly tender, 3 to 5 minutes. Remove from heat and cool to room temperature. In a small bowl combine cheese with thyme, salt and pepper.

To assemble, spoon mushroom mixture evenly over crust. Using a spatula, distribute cheese mixture evenly over mushrooms. Sprinkle remaining garlic over top. Bake for 10 to 12 minutes, until warmed through. Let sit for at least 10 minutes before serving.

Makes 8 appetizer servings.

APRICOT AND JALAPENO CHEESE TORTE
Feasts of Fancy Catering

8 ounces dried apricots, chopped

6 (8 ounce) packages cream
  cheese, softened

1 small red onion, minced

1/2 cup jalapeno jelly, plus
  2 tablespoons for topping

Salt and pepper to taste

Cilantro leaves, for garnish

Line a 9-inch spring form pan with plastic wrap leaving enough to fold over the top. Using a food processor, process the chopped apricots. They will "gather" and form a ball. With a rolling pin roll apricots out to form a circle that is slightly larger than the pan. Place the rolled apricots into the pan. Using an electric mixer, combine cream cheese, onion, 1/2 cup of the jelly and salt and pepper. Mix on low speed until creamy. Spoon the cheese mixture evenly over the apricot layer and pat down. Cover with the excess plastic wrap and refrigerate overnight. When ready to serve, invert onto serving plate. Spread remaining jelly over apricot top. Top with cilantro leaves.

Makes 50 servings.

DOC'S DIP
K C Masterpiece Barbecue & Grill

4 tablespoons butter
1/2 cup chopped onions
6 tablespoons all-purpose flour
1 cup milk
1/2 teaspoon chicken soup base
1/8 teaspoon white pepper
1 teaspoon seasoned salt
1/4 cup picante sauce
12 ounces cream cheese
1 (14 1/2-ounce) can diced
   tomatoes, drained
1 (10-ounce) box frozen chopped
   spinach, thawed and drained
2 tablespoons sherry

In a saucepan melt butter over medium heat and sauté onions until transparent. In a container with a tight fitting lid thoroughly mix the flour and milk and add to the onion mixture. Stir constantly until thickened and remove from heat. In a separate container mix soup base, white pepper, seasoned salt and picante sauce until dissolved. Add to the onion and flour mixture; mix thoroughly. Cook over low heat until thoroughly warm. Transfer mixture to a blender. Add cream cheese, tomatoes, spinach and sherry. Blend until smooth. Refrigerate until ready to serve, then place dip in an ovenproof dish. Bake at 350 degrees for 30 minutes. Serve hot.

Makes 5 cups.

BEEF EMPANADAS
Piropos

Empanada Dough
3 1/2 cups all-purpose flour
1 tablespoon salt
3/8 cup vegetable shortening
Water (as needed)

Beef Filling
2 tablespoons oil
2 large yellow onions, chopped
1/4 pound green onion, sliced
1/2 cup raisins
5 green olives, pitted and chopped
1 teaspoon oregano
1 teaspoon cumin
1 tablespoon aji molido or mild
  red pepper flakes
  (available in specialty food stores)
1 pound ground beef
1 teaspoon salt
1 teaspoon black pepper

CHEF'S NOTE
If you cannot find mild red pepper flakes, you can substitute red pepper flakes but adjust the quantity so that filling is not too hot.

For the dough, in a large bowl mix the flour and salt. Make a hole in center of mixture and add shortening and water gradually. Work the dough until it doesn't stick to your fingers and the dough is soft. Let sit for one hour. Using a rolling pin, roll out the dough on a lightly floured surface and fold in half. Roll again to 1/8-inch thickness. Cut into 5-inch circles.

For the filling, in a skillet heat oil over medium heat and sauté onions until transparent. Add raisins, olives, oregano, cumin and aji molido. Add ground beef and cook over low heat about 10 minutes until beef is thoroughly browned. Drain off the excess fat. Add salt and pepper.

To assemble empanadas, place 1/4 to 1/2 cup of filling on each circle of dough. Fold over, being careful not to stretch the dough. Crimp edges. Deep fat fry at 350 degrees just until golden brown.

Makes 10 servings.

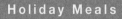

Holiday Meals

Added expense during the holiday season can further stress an already stretched food budget. While Harvesters focuses on making food available to those in need all year long, the organization recognizes the important role food plays in many holiday traditions. The goal of Harvesters' Holiday Meal program is to provide a special holiday meal for every person in need. Through the program, Harvesters purchases and collects donations of turkeys, hams, baking hens and food accompaniments for distribution to member agencies that serve people in need. Beyond just nourishing the body, traditional holiday meals strengthen the bonds of family and community, and provide hope for better tomorrows.

...the main event

GRILLED ATLANTIC MACKEREL WITH SUMMER HEIRLOOM TOMATOES AND PANCETTA STUDDED MASHED POTATOES
40 Sardines

4 (4-ounce) pieces mackerel
1/4 cup extra virgin olive oil, divided
2 cloves garlic, thinly sliced, divided
Salt and pepper to taste
1 cup diced pancetta
8 Yukon Gold potatoes, peeled
4 tablespoons butter
1 bunch scallions, minced
Leaves from 3 sprigs of
    fresh thyme
Leaves from 3 sprigs of fresh basil
Leaves from 5 sprigs of fresh
    oregano
2 yellow heirloom tomatoes,
    each sliced into 4 thick slices
2 red heirloom tomatoes,
    each sliced into 4 thick slices
Fresh cracked black pepper
4 sprigs fresh basil for garnish

**Wine Suggestion:
Dashe Sangiovese,
Sonoma County**

Rub mackerel with 2 tablespoons olive oil and 1 sliced clove of garlic. Season with salt and pepper and set aside. In a skillet cook pancetta over medium heat until lightly browned and crisp. Drain and set aside. In a large pan boil the potatoes until soft. Drain and mash with a fork. Add butter, scallions and pancetta. Season with salt and pepper. Set aside and keep warm. In a small bowl combine the thyme, basil and oregano. Season each tomato slice with the second sliced garlic clove, fresh herb mix, salt and pepper. Place a sheet of aluminum foil on the grill and brush it with olive oil. Grill the mackerel on both sides until done as desired. Grill the tomatoes until they begin to soften. To serve, arrange one red tomato slice and one yellow tomato slice in the center of each plate. Place a piece of mackerel on the tomatoes. Set a small scoop of potatoes next to the mackerel. Drizzle with remaining olive oil. Sprinkle pepper over plate, garnish with basil. Serve immediately.

Makes 4 servings.

PAN ROASTED SCALLOPS WITH ENGLISH PEA PANCAKES AND FOREST MUSHROOM RAGOUT

The American Restaurant

Pancakes
1/2 cup shelled English peas
3/4 cup whole milk
1 egg, well beaten
2 tablespoons butter, melted
3/4 teaspoon kosher salt
Freshly ground black pepper to taste
Pinch baking powder
1/2 cup all-purpose flour

Mushroom Ragout
1 teaspoon olive oil
2 cups morels or other forest
   mushrooms
1 shallot, finely diced
1 clove garlic, finely diced
1/2 cup mushroom or
   vegetable stock
1 tablespoon butter, cold
Kosher salt to taste
Freshly ground black pepper to taste

Scallops
2 tablespoons olive oil
Salt and freshly ground black pepper
   to taste
16 jumbo scallops

For the pancakes, blanch peas in heavily salted water. In a blender purée the peas with the milk until smooth. Add egg, butter, salt, pepper and baking powder and combine. Slowly add flour until mixture is the consistency of pancake batter. In a heavy bottom sauté pan over medium high heat, drop spoonfuls of batter to form pancakes about 2 inches in diameter. Cook until lightly browned. Makes 16 pancakes.

For the ragout, in a sauté pan heat the olive oil over medium high heat. Add the mushrooms and sauté for about 45 seconds. Add shallots and garlic and cook until golden brown. Add stock, butter, salt and pepper, stirring to combine. Adjust seasoning.

For the scallops, season to taste with salt and pepper. In a sauté pan heat the olive oil over medium high heat, add the scallops and sear, cooking a minute and a half on each side. To serve, place 4 pancakes on each plate, top each with a scallop and add a spoonful of the mushroom ragout.

Makes 4 servings.

SPICE RUBBED HALIBUT WITH SAUTÉED RAPINI
The Capital Grille

Spice Rub

1/4 cup whole mustard seed

1/4 cup whole black peppercorns

1/4 cup whole fennel

1/4 cup whole coriander

1/3 cup granulated garlic

1/4 cup paprika

1/4 cup kosher salt

1/4 cup celery salt

Halibut

11 ounces Atlantic halibut

1 tablespoon extra virgin olive oil

2 teaspoons spice rub

1 tablespoon butter

2 ounces rapini, blanched
   and finely chopped

1/4 ounce bacon, cooked and diced

Salt and pepper to taste

2 teaspoons balsamic glaze
   (available in specialty food stores)

1 lemon wrap, for garnish

Parsley sprig, for garnish

For the spice rub, in a sauté pan over high heat toast the mustard seeds, peppercorns, fennel and coriander for 3 to 4 minutes until fragrant and lightly toasted in color. Cool and grind finely in a spice grinder. Add garlic, paprika, salt and celery salt. Mix well. Store covered in dry storage.

For the halibut, place halibut on a baking sheet and brush with olive oil. Season flesh side with spice rub. Roast at 400 degrees for 10 to 12 minutes, until just done. Meanwhile, in a sauté pan melt butter and sauté rapini with bacon. Season with salt and pepper. To serve, place rapini on back of plate. Place fish over part of the rapini, letting some green show. Drizzle balsamic glaze over fish. Garnish with lemon and parsley.

Makes 2 servings.

**Wine Suggestion:
Domaine Vieux
Telegraphe
Chateauneuf du
Pape Blanc**

BLACKENED CATFISH A LA MER

Jazz – A Louisiana Kitchen

Sauce
1 teaspoon unsalted butter
1/2 teaspoon chopped garlic
1/2 cup chopped green onions
1/2 pound medium shrimp,
   peeled and deveined
1/2 pound lump crabmeat
1/2 cup seafood stock or water
1 pint heavy whipping cream
Seafood seasoning to taste
8 ounces freshly grated
   parmesan cheese

Catfish
6 (6-ounce) catfish filets
2 tablespoons margarine, melted
2 tablespoons blackening or
   Cajun seasoning, plus additional
   to taste

For the sauce, in a two-quart saucepan melt butter and add garlic, green onions, shrimp and crab. Sauté until lightly browned. Add seafood stock and cook until shrimp are pink. Lower heat and add whipping cream. Bring to a gentle boil, stirring constantly. Add seafood seasoning to taste. Add parmesan cheese and stir until thickened. Set aside and keep warm.

For the catfish, heat a cast iron skillet or griddle over high heat. Coat the catfish thoroughly with margarine and blackening seasoning. Add filets to skillet and sear on one side until the edges are white. Turn and continue to cook until completely cooked, but still moist. Be careful not to overcook, as skillet will be extremely hot. Place each catfish filet on a plate and cover with sauce.

Makes 6 servings.

CHEF'S NOTE
Fish can be served over a bed of dirty or white rice.

31

LOBSTER ARMORICAINE
Hannah Bistro Café

1 (2 1/4-pound) lobster

1/4 cup (1/2 stick) butter, at room temperature

1 teaspoon finely chopped chervil

1 teaspoon minced parsley

1 teaspoon finely chopped tarragon

1/4 cup plus 2 tablespoons canola oil

1 medium shallot, peeled and finely chopped

1 clove garlic, whole

1/2 cup cognac

3/4 cup plus 2 tablespoons white wine such as muscadet

2 medium vine-ripened tomatoes, peeled and chopped

Cayenne pepper to taste

Salt to taste

1/4 cup good-quality champagne

CHEF'S NOTE

Serve with fresh asparagus and fettucine or mashed potatoes.

Place the lobster on a cutting board and split lengthwise. Remove and reserve all of the green matter (tomalley) in the head. Tear off tail. Tear off claws and cut in half. Split knuckles lengthwise. Remove gills from body and discard. In a small bowl combine tomalley, butter, chervil, parsley and tarragon. Set aside. In a sauté pan over medium-high heat, heat the oil and sauté the lobster pieces until they redden. Add the shallot, garlic, cognac, wine, tomatoes, cayenne pepper and salt. Sprinkle with the champagne and flame. Reduce heat to medium and continue to cook for 20 minutes. Remove the lobster pieces to a serving dish. Discard the body and legs. Cook the sauce over high heat until reduced by half. Stir in the butter mixture and continue to cook until sauce is of creamy consistency. Coat the lobster with the sauce and serve.

Makes 2 servings.

POULET SAUTÉ AU HERB
Tatsu's French Restaurant

---

4 pieces of boneless chicken,
   thigh or breast, skin on
Salt and pepper to taste
1/4 cup all-purpose flour
2 tablespoons vegetable oil
2 tablespoons unsalted butter
1/8 teaspoon sugar
1/8 teaspoon oregano
1/8 teaspoon thyme
1/8 teaspoon ground black pepper
1/8 teaspoon rosemary
1/8 teaspoon garlic powder
1/8 teaspoon chives
Juice of 1/4 lemon

Season chicken pieces with salt and pepper and coat with flour. In a skillet heat oil over medium heat. Place chicken pieces skin side down and sauté until skin is dark and crisp. Turn pieces over and cook just until done. Remove chicken from skillet and pour off excess oil. Return skillet to medium heat. Add unsalted butter along with sugar, oregano, thyme, pepper, rosemary, garlic powder and chives. Heat until butter is melted and blended with herbs. Add chicken pieces and turn until coated with the warm herb mixture. Squeeze lemon juice over all and serve.

Makes 2 to 4 servings.

**Wine Suggestion:
Gundlach
Bundschu
Chardonnay**

JJ's CHICKEN MARSALA
JJ's

4 (6-ounce) boneless
   chicken breasts
1/4 cup all-purpose flour
8 teaspoons butter
6 ounces dry Marsala wine
1/2 cup sliced button mushrooms
6 ounces heavy whipping cream
1/2 tablespoon chopped
   red pimientos
1/2 tablespoon chopped
   green onions
Salt and coarse ground
   black pepper to taste

Dust chicken breasts with flour.
In a 12-inch skillet melt butter over
medium heat. Add chicken breasts
and sauté until almost fully cooked.
Add wine and mushrooms. Increase
heat gradually and reduce by half.
Add whipping cream, pimientos,
green onions, salt and pepper.
Stir to mix well. Reduce until
mixture thickens.

Makes 4 servings.

**Wine Suggestion:
Gagliardo
Dolcetto D'Alba**

CHEF'S NOTE
*Serve with sautéed
vegetables and wild
rice or mashed
potatoes.*

ROAST DUCKLING WITH PEPPERCORN SAUCE
Eddy's Catering

Roast Duckling

1 (4-pound) duckling, rinsed
 inside and out

3 tablespoons salt, divided

2 oranges, quartered

4 sprigs thyme

1 teaspoon white pepper

1 teaspoon anise powder
 (may substitute fennel seed)

2 tablespoons dried rosemary

2 tablespoons paprika

Peppercorn Sauce

1 tablespoon green peppercorns

1/4 cup brandy

3 cups beef stock, or equal parts
 duck stock and veal glaze

2 teaspoons Worcestershire sauce

1 tablespoon balsamic vinegar

2 tablespoons butter

2 tablespoons all-purpose flour

**Wine Suggestion:
Storybook
Mayacamus
Zinfandel**

Preheat oven to 375 degrees. Sprinkle 1 teaspoon salt inside duck. Place oranges and thyme in cavity. Combine remaining salt, pepper, anise, rosemary and paprika; rub entire surface of duck. Place in pan and bake for 15 to 20 minutes. Reduce temperature to 275 degrees and continue roasting for 90 minutes or until leg separates easily from duck.

For the sauce, in a saucepan place peppercorns and brandy and heat over medium heat until reduced by half. Add beef stock, Worcestershire sauce and vinegar and bring to a boil. In a small sauté pan melt butter and stir in flour. Cook briefly. Add flour mixture to liquid a small amount at a time, stirring vigorously until sauce is thickened. Cool duck to room temperature. Preheat oven to 450 degrees. Make two cuts on either side of breast bone about 1/4-inch apart. Slide fingers along cuts and remove breast and leg in one piece. Place in oven for 10 minutes, until skin is crispy. Slice and serve with sauce.

Makes 2 to 3 servings.

ROASTED RACK OF LAMB WITH ROASTED TOMATO JUS
Joe D's Winebar Café and Patio

2 eight-rib racks of lamb, frenched
Salt and pepper to taste
1/4 cup extra virgin olive oil, divided
8 cloves of garlic, roasted, divided
2 tablespoons butter, at room
  temperature, divided
2 sprigs of thyme
1 cup veal stock (available in
  specialty food store)
10 tomatoes, halved, roasted and
  finely chopped

Preheat oven to 425 degrees. Season the lamb with salt and pepper. In a roasting pan heat 1 tablespoon olive oil over medium-high heat. Place lamb in pan and sear on all sides. Rub lamb with 4 of the garlic cloves and 1/2 tablespoon of the butter. Tuck sprigs of thyme underneath. Place lamb in oven and roast 9 minutes for medium rare. Remove from oven and let rest. Pour off the fat and discard thyme. Add the stock, scraping the drippings from the bottom of the pan. Add the remaining cloves of garlic and the tomatoes. Simmer until slightly thickened; strain. Stir in remaining olive oil and butter.

Makes 4 servings.

CHEF'S NOTE
Serve with morels, asparagus, roasted tomatoes and roasted garlic cloves.

ROASTED LAMB SHANKS WITH QUESO FRESCO
The Grille on Broadway

1 small summer squash, chopped
1 small rutabaga, chopped
1 small potato, chopped
1 carrot, chopped
1 rib celery, chopped
1/2 jalapeno pepper, chopped
    and seeded
4 large lamb shanks
2 beef bouillon cubes
1 cup red wine
1 sprig of rosemary
1/2 teaspoon thyme
1 bay leaf
Salt and pepper to taste
1/2 cup shredded queso fresco
    or Monterey Jack cheese

In a deep roasting pan, place all the vegetables. Add lamb shanks, bouillon and red wine. Add water, just to cover. Add rosemary, thyme, bay leaf, and salt and pepper to taste. Cover tightly. Place in a 300-degree oven and bake for 4 to 5 hours until the shanks are tender. Remove from oven. Separate the shanks and vegetables, reserving the liquid. In a blender container, purée the vegetables with 1/4 cup of the reserved broth. Let vegetables sit for about ten minutes to cool slightly. To serve, spoon vegetable purée into a mound in the center of a large serving platter. Top with the shanks and ladle the broth around the outer edge. Sprinkle the cheese over the shanks and allow to melt.

Makes 4 servings.

**Wine Suggestion:
2001 Marston
Family Vineyards
Napa Cabernet
Sauvignon**

OSSOBUCO di VITELLO
Lidia Bastianich – Lidia's Kansas City

2 veal hindshanks, split in two
   and tied widthwise
Salt and freshly ground pepper
   to taste
1 cup all-purpose flour
1/2 cup vegetable oil
2 celery stalks, cut in large chunks
2 carrots, cut in large chunks
2 onions, cut in large chunks
2 sprigs fresh rosemary
2 bay leaves
4 whole cloves
2 tablespoons tomato paste
1 cup white wine
1 cup San Marzano tomatoes,
   crushed
1/2 cup orange juice
Zest of 1 orange
Zest of 1 lemon
4 cups chicken stock

**Wine Suggestion:
Badia Coltibuono
Chianti Classico
Riserva**

Season the veal shanks liberally with salt and pepper. Dredge in the flour and shake off excess. In a heavy braising pan heat the vegetable oil and brown the shanks on all sides. Remove from pan and set aside. In the same pan, sauté the celery, carrot and onion until they begin to wilt. Tie the rosemary, bay leaves and cloves into a small piece of cheesecloth and add to the pan. Add the tomato paste and cook until the vegetables are well coated and the paste begins to caramelize. Add the white wine and cook until almost evaporated. Add the crushed tomato, orange juice, orange zest, lemon zest and chicken stock and bring to a boil. Return the veal shanks to the pan, cover tightly and braise in a 350-degree oven for approximately two hours until tender. Remove the ossobuco from the braising liquid, untie them, and place in a serving dish. Pass the braising liquid and vegetables through a sieve to make the sauce. Adjust the consistency of the sauce by reducing if necessary. Return the shanks to the sauce and keep warm until ready to serve.

Makes 4 servings.

RICH DAVIS' BARBECUED PORK TENDERLOIN

KC Masterpiece Barbecue & Grill

3 large pork tenderloins,
   at room temperature

Marinade
1 cup soy sauce
1/3 cup sesame oil
3 large garlic cloves, minced
1 tablespoon ground ginger

Sauce
1 (18-ounce) bottle KC
   Masterpiece Barbecue Sauce®
1/3 cup soy sauce
1/4 cup sesame oil
1 garlic clove, minced

In a small bowl combine marinade ingredients. Place tenderloins in glass or enameled pan. Pour marinade over meat, cover with plastic wrap and let marinate overnight in the refrigerator. Place tenderloins on a charcoal grill (with seasoned hickory chips added to smoke) over indirect low fire. Cook with lid closed, turning every 15 minutes and basting with marinade, about 1 1/2 hours.

For the sauce, in a saucepan combine barbecue sauce, soy sauce, sesame oil and garlic. Heat thoroughly and serve with meat.

Makes 6 to 8 servings.

**Wine Suggestion:
On the Edge
Zinfandel,
Frediani Vineyard**

PORK LOIN WITH APRICOT GLAZE
Doubletree

1 (4-pound) center cut pork loin
2 tablespoons all-purpose rub
1 tablespoon butter
1 tablespoon chopped shallots
1 teaspoon chopped garlic
6 dried apricots, chopped
1/4 cup peach schnapps
1/4 cup apricot jam

Preheat oven to 350 degrees. Season pork loin with all-purpose rub and place in roasting pan. Place in oven and roast for 40 minutes. Meanwhile in a sauté pan melt butter and sweat shallots and garlic. Add apricots and schnapps. Flame, then add jam and mix well. Brush about 2 to 3 tablespoons glaze over the pork loin and cook for an additional 15 minutes. Slice and serve with remaining glaze.

Makes 8 servings.

Wine Suggestion: Kangarilla Road Shiraz

FILET MEDALLIONS WITH BALSAMIC AND MADEIRA WINE SAUCE

Hereford House

---

2 tablespoons cooking oil

4 (6-ounce) beef filets

1 yellow onion, julienned

1 bell pepper, julienned

1 cup mushrooms, sliced

2 ounces smoked bacon,
diced and cooked

1 teaspoon minced shallots

2 cups Madeira wine

6 tablespoons balsamic vinegar

4 ounces veal demi-glace
(available in specialty food stores)

6 tablespoons salted butter

Wine Suggestion: Lang and Reed Cabernet Franc, Premier Etage

In a large skillet heat the cooking oil over high heat. Place filets in the skillet and cook to desired temperature. The exterior of the filets should be well seared (dark brown). Remove the steaks and place them in a warm oven (140 degrees) until ready to serve. In the same skillet sauté the onion, pepper, mushrooms, bacon and shallots over medium heat until the onions are caramelized. Add the Madeira wine and vinegar. Reduce by half (use caution as the wine will flame for 30 to 60 seconds). Add the veal glaze and reduce by half again. Remove the skillet from the heat and finish by whisking in the butter until well incorporated. Ladle over filets.

Makes 4 servings.

STUFFED PORK LOIN WITH BRANDIED PEPPERCORN CREAM AND CARAMELIZED ONION AND PANCETTA

Paulo & Bill's

Stuffed Pork Loin
1 gallon water
1/4 cup salt
1/4 cup sugar
1 orange, quartered
1 teaspoon crushed red pepper
1 (3-pound) boneless pork loin
2 cups chopped fresh spinach
1 cup goat cheese
1/4 cup sliced toasted almonds
1/4 cup raisins

Brandied Peppercorn Cream
1/2 tablespoon butter
3 shallots, sliced
1/4 cup brandy
1 cup chicken stock
1 cup veal stock
1 quart heavy whipping cream
Salt and freshly cracked
    black pepper to taste

Caramelized Onion and Pancetta
1/2 cup julienned pancetta
1 yellow onion, sliced

In a large stockpot over high heat combine the water, salt, sugar, orange and red pepper. Bring to a boil, then remove from heat and cool completely. Pour over pork loin and refrigerate for 24 hours.

Cut pork loin lengthwise, 3/4 of the way through. Make a second cut horizontally half way through remaining section of pork. Lay out flat, cover with plastic wrap and pound meat until it is of uniform thickness. In a large bowl combine the spinach, goat cheese, almonds and raisins. Mix thoroughly by hand. Place stuffing across top third of pork. Roll the rest of the pork on top of the stuffing. Tie with butcher's twine. Sear the pork in a hot skillet then place in a 325-degree oven for 30 minutes. Let rest for 15 minutes before slicing.

For the peppercorn cream, in a sauté pan over medium-high heat melt the butter and sweat the shallots. Add brandy and reduce by half. Add chicken stock, veal stock and whipping cream. Continue cooking over low heat; reduce until thickened. Season to taste with salt and pepper.

For the caramelized onion and pancetta, in a sauté pan over low heat render pancetta until crispy. Remove pancetta from pan, leaving the fat. Increase heat to medium, add onions and cook until golden brown, about 15 to 20 minutes, stirring occasionally. Stir pancetta back into onions.

To serve, top slices of pork loin with the peppercorn cream. Place the caramelized onions and pancetta on the side.

Makes 6 to 8 servings.

**Wine Suggestion:
Susana Balbo
Estate Malbec**

HERB CRUSTED FILET MIGNON WITH RED WINE SHALLOT DEMI-GLACE

Morton's, The Steakhouse – Kansas City

4 (10 to 14-ounce) filet mignons
4 tablespoons clarified butter
Seasoning salt

Herb Coating Mix
1 cup (2 sticks) butter,
   at room temperature
2 tablespoons puréed garlic
3/4 cup minced parsley
1/4 cup minced fresh basil
1/4 cup minced chives
3/4 cup dried breadcrumbs

Red Wine Shallot Demi-Glace
2 tablespoons clarified butter
1/4 cup chopped shallots
2 whole garlic cloves
1/4 tablespoon chopped
   thyme leaves
1 bay leaf
3 cups red wine
4 cups reconstituted demi-glace
   (available at specialty food stores)
3 tablespoons butter,
   at room temperature

For the herb coating, in a mixing bowl blend all ingredients. Set aside.

For the wine demi-glace, in a large saucepan heat the clarified butter. Sauté the shallots and garlic until shallots are soft. Add the cloves, thyme, bay leaf and red wine. Bring mixture to a boil and reduce until mixture is thick and bubbling. Add the demi-glace and continue to reduce down to 2 cups. Strain the sauce and return to the sauté pan. Over low heat, whip in the softened butter so that the sauce is very shiny.

Preheat oven to 500 degrees. Season steaks with seasoning salt, and roll in herb coating mix. In a sauté pan, heat the clarified butter. Add steaks and brown on all sides. Move steaks to a baking sheet and place in oven for 15 to 20 minutes. To serve, pour wine demi-glace onto plate and place filet on top.

Makes 4 servings.

DRY-AGED BONELESS RIB-EYE STEAKS WITH GREEN PEPPERCORN SAUCE

The Capital Grille

1/4 cup Corvoisier brandy

2 tablespoons green peppercorns in brine, drained and rinsed

1 tablespoon paper-thin sliced shallots

2 cups reconstituted beef demi-glace (available at specialty food stores)

1 pound fresh porcini mushrooms, sliced

Kosher salt to taste

Freshly cracked black pepper to taste

6 (20-ounce) dry-aged rib-eye steaks

Seasoned salt

Watercress, for garnish

In a medium saucepan heat the brandy and flame to cook off the alcohol. Add the peppercorns and shallots to the brandy and simmer for 2 minutes. Add demi-glace and mushrooms and simmer for twenty minutes, until mixture coats back of spoon. Add salt and pepper to taste. Remove from heat and set aside. Season the steaks with seasoned salt on all sides and cook to desired temperature. To serve, place the steak in the center of a warm dinner plate. Top with peppercorn sauce. Garnish with watercress.

Makes 6 servings.

Wine Suggestion: Neyers Napa Valley Merlot

HONEY SOY GLAZED SHORT RIBS WITH PINEAPPLE AND MANGO CHUTNEY
Le Fou Frog

Short Ribs

1/4 cup vegetable oil

3 onions, large dice

2 carrots, large dice

2 celery stalks, large dice

2 pounds beef short ribs

1/2 cup tomato paste

1 cup hearty red wine

1 bulb garlic, split into cloves

3 bay leaves, crumbled

1 tablespoon chopped fresh thyme

8 black peppercorns

Honey Soy Glaze

1/4 cup soy sauce

1 tablespoon yellow curry
(available in Vietnamese markets
or specialty food stores)

1 tablespoon crushed red
pepper flakes

1 cup honey

Chutney

1 teaspoon oil

1/2 cup diced mango

1/2 cup diced pineapple

1 tablespoon grated ginger

2 tablespoons sugar

2 tablespoons rice wine vinegar

In a roasting pan heat the oil over medium heat. Sauté the onions, carrots and celery until soft. Add the ribs and brown on all sides. Add the tomato paste and the wine; stir to deglaze the pan. Add enough water to cover the meat, then add the garlic, bay leaves, thyme and peppercorns. Cover the pan and place in 350-degree oven. Cook for 2 to 3 hours until ribs are tender and meat is falling off the bone.

For the glaze, in a saucepan bring soy sauce, curry and pepper flakes to boil over high heat. Add honey, turn heat to low, allow to reduce for about 10 minutes. Remove from heat.

For the chutney, in a saucepan heat the oil over medium heat. Add the mango, pineapple, ginger and sugar and cook until the fruit is tender. Add the vinegar and continue to cook over low heat until the vinegar has been absorbed by the fruit.

Remove ribs from pan and coat with glaze. Place under broiler for 1 - 2 minutes. Watch carefully that glaze does not caramelize. Serve with chutney.

Makes 4 servings.

BOBOTIE
Classic Cup

2 tablespoons butter

2 tablespoons vegetable oil

2 medium white or yellow onions, diced

1/2 teaspoon crushed garlic

1 tablespoon curry powder

2 1/4 pounds minced lamb or beef, or a mixture of the two

2 slices bread, torn into pieces

1/4 cup milk

Finely grated rind and juice of 1/2 lemon

1 egg

Salt and pepper to taste

4 ounces apricots, chopped

1 tart green apple, such as Granny Smith, peeled, cored and diced

1/4 cup golden raisins

2 ounces slivered almonds, roasted

6 fresh lemon, orange or bay leaves

Topping

1 cup milk

2 eggs

1/2 teaspoon salt, or to taste

Preheat oven to 350 degrees. In a saucepan heat the butter and oil and sauté the onions and garlic until translucent. Stir in the curry powder and cook briefly until fragrant. Remove from heat. Add the lamb or beef and mix well. In a large bowl combine the bread, milk, lemon juice, lemon rind, egg, salt, pepper, apricots, apple, raisins and almonds. Combine with meat mixture. Place all into a buttered casserole and level the top. Roll up the leaves and bury them throughout the casserole, distributing evenly. Seal with foil and bake 1 hour. Increase the oven temperature to 400 degrees. In a small bowl, mix the topping ingredients. Pour over the casserole and bake for another 15 minutes, uncovered.

Makes 8 servings.

Wine Suggestion: Neil Ellis Shiraz

POLENTA CON RAGU DI SALSICCIA E PEPERONATA
Baked Polenta Casserole with a Ragu of Spicy Sausage and Sweet Peppers
Milano

Sausage Ragout
1/4 cup extra virgin olive oil
1 small onion, chopped
2 tablespoons chopped garlic
1 pound bulk Italian sausage
1 red bell pepper, chopped
1 yellow bell pepper, chopped
1 green bell pepper, chopped
1 sprig fresh rosemary, chopped
1 bay leaf
Salt to taste
Red chili flakes to taste
1 cup red wine, preferably Chianti
1 (28-ounce) can tomatoes
1/2 cup freshly grated
   parmigiano-reggiano cheese

Polenta
1 quart water
Kosher salt to taste
4 tablespoons unsalted butter,
   divided
1 cup cornmeal
1 sprig fresh rosemary, chopped
3 fresh sage leaves, chopped
1/2 cup freshly grated
   parmigiano-reggiano cheese
Additional (about 3/4 cup) grated
   parmigiano-reggiano cheese,
   for layering and topping

For the sausage ragu, in a large saucepan heat the olive oil over medium high heat. Add onion and garlic and sauté until softened, 4 to 5 minutes. Add Italian sausage, brown, breaking it up and cooking it thoroughly, about 10 minutes. Add the peppers, rosemary and bay leaf. Season with salt and red chili flakes. Sauté 3 to 4 minutes, stirring often. Add the red wine, scraping the bottom of the pan with a wooden spoon to release any browned particles into the sauce. Reduce the red wine by half. Add the tomatoes, reduce heat to low and simmer, covered, for one hour. Add cheese and additional salt to taste.

48

For the polenta, in a 2-quart saucepan bring salted water to a boil with 1 tablespoon of the butter. Slowly add cornmeal in a fine trickle, stirring constantly with a whisk. Stir in rosemary and sage. Reduce heat to low and simmer, covered, for 45 minutes, stirring occasionally. Remove from heat. Using a whisk, whip in the remaining butter and the cheese. Add additional salt to taste, if desired.

To assemble, in a casserole dish layer the sausage ragu and the polenta, making two to three layers of each and sprinkling more cheese between each layer. Finish by topping with additional cheese. Bake at 350 degrees for 20 to 30 minutes until hot and bubbling. Let stand for 5 minutes before serving.

Makes 6 to 8 servings.

Wine Suggestion: Guerrieri Rizzardi Valpolicella Pojega

TORTELLINI ALLA PANNA TARTUFATA
Meat-filled Tortellini in White Truffle Cream Sauce
Milano

1 1/2 pounds meat-filled tortellini
1 1/2 cups heavy cream
3 tablespoons butter
1/2 cup freshly grated
    parmigiano-reggiano cheese
1 tablespoon white truffle oil
    (available at specialty Italian
    food stores)
Salt to taste

In a large pot bring salted water to a boil. Add tortellini and cook until tender, about 3 to 7 minutes depending on size. Meanwhile, in a large sauté pan bring cream to a simmer over medium high heat. Reduce until slightly thickened, approximately 3 to 4 minutes. Add butter and melt into cream. Drain cooked pasta, reserving a bit of the cooking water, and add to the cream sauce. Stir to combine. Add cheese, white truffle oil, and salt to taste. If cream sauce becomes too thick, thin with some of the reserved pasta water to desired consistency. Serve immediately in warm bowls, offering additional cheese as desired.

Makes 8 servings.

CHEF'S NOTE
Make with cheese-filled tortellini for a delightful vegetarian dish.

SEAFOOD MACARONI AND CHEESE
McCormick and Schmick's

1 teaspoon garlic

1 teaspoon oil

2 cups heavy cream

1 pinch salt

1 pinch white pepper

1 (1-pound) block processed American cheese

1 (16-ounce) bag macaroni, cooked

1 1/2 cups parmesan cheese, divided

1 pound cooked seafood (any combination of peeled shrimp, crabmeat or scallops)

1 cup bread crumbs

In a heavy bottom saucepan over low heat, sweat garlic in oil for 1 minute. Add cream, salt and pepper and bring almost to a simmer. Turn the heat as low as possible and slowly add the processed cheese, stirring constantly until all cheese is added and melted. Add the cooked macaroni, 1 cup of the parmesan cheese and the seafood and continue to stir over low heat until warmed through. Transfer to a casserole dish and top with the remaining 1/2 cup parmesan cheese and the breadcrumbs. Bake at 350 degrees for about 10 to 15 minutes or until top is browned and bubbling.

Makes 4 to 6 servings.

**Wine Suggestion:
Domaine Talmard
Macon Chardonnay**

NUTRITION EDUCATION

Stretching food resources to meet the nutritional needs of low-income families takes knowledge and skill. Harvesters' Project STRENGTH helps participants do just that. The eight-week course curriculum covers important nutrition basics, food safety and hands-on cooking. Participants learn the art of menu planning, budgeting and comparative shopping. The program also fosters a forum for social interaction, inspiration and problem solving.

Project STRENGTH helps to bridge the gap between assistance and self-sufficiency.

...on the side

BUTTERNUT SQUASH SOUP
The Grille on Broadway

2 tablespoons vegetable oil
1 tablespoon minced garlic
1 large carrot, minced
1 jalapeno pepper, seeded
 and chopped
2 stalks celery, minced
1 large onion, minced
2 butternut squash, peeled,
 seeded and chopped
1/4 cup dry sherry
1/4 cup cream cheese
Salt and pepper to taste
Shredded raw carrot, for garnish
Nutmeg or cayenne pepper,
 for garnish

In a large saucepan over medium heat, heat the oil and sauté garlic, carrot, jalapeno, celery and onion until celery and onion are translucent. Add squash and water to cover. Bring to a boil, reduce heat and simmer until squash is tender, about 30 minutes. Remove from heat. Transfer the mixture in batches to a blender and purée until smooth. Return to the saucepan and add sherry, cream cheese and salt and pepper to taste. Stir over low heat until blended. Serve garnished with shredded carrot and a sprinkle of nutmeg or cayenne pepper.

Makes 6 servings.

CHEF'S NOTE
Vegetable or chicken broth can be substituted for the water. If so, reduce the salt.

CHICKEN, ESCAROLE AND TORTELLINI SOUP

Frondizi's Ristorante

1 (3-pound) chicken

1 bay leaf

2 large onions, diced

5 stalks celery, diced

3 carrots, diced

1 head of escarole, separated
    into leaves and blanched

1 bag frozen tortellini, cooked
    and drained

Freshly grated parmesan cheese
    or extra virgin olive oil,
    for garnish (optional)

In a large stockpot cover the chicken with water and boil with the bay leaf for 1 hour or until tender and easily pulled from the bone. Remove chicken from the broth. Add the onions, celery and carrots to the broth and simmer until tender. Pull chicken meat from the bones, chop and put back into the soup. Simmer 5 minutes. Place 1 or 2 escarole leaves and 5 or 6 tortellini in each serving bowl. Ladle hot soup into bowls. Garnish with grated parmesan cheese or olive oil if desired.

Makes 8 servings.

R.T.'s TANGY BACHELOR VEGETABLE SOUP
Salsman Catering and Event Planners

---

2 beef shanks

2 medium shallots, chopped

2 stalks celery, cut into
 bite-size pieces

2 carrots, cut into
 bite-size pieces

2 potatoes, cut into
 bite-size pieces

1 (10-ounce) package frozen peas

1 (10-ounce) package frozen
 green beans

1/4 cup barley

Pinch basil

1 1/2 cups bottled Bloody Mary mix

In a large pot 2/3 full of water, combine shanks, shallots, celery, carrots, potatoes, peas, beans, barley and basil. Add the Bloody Mary mix. Cook soup over low heat for about 3 hours or until meat falls off the bones. Remove the bones and discard. Chop meat into bite-size pieces and return to soup.

Makes 4 servings.

CHEF'S NOTE
While soup is cooking, make yourself a Bloody Mary – sit back and enjoy the game!

LOBSTER BISQUE
Savoy Grill

Meat from 3 pounds of boiled live
   lobster, chopped; shells, body,
   tomalley and 1 cup cooking
   liquid reserved
2 tablespoons olive oil
1 medium onion, chopped
1/2 celery stalk, chopped
1 carrot, chopped
1 tomato, chopped
1 head garlic, halved crosswise
2 tablespoons chopped, fresh
   tarragon leaves
2 tablespoons chopped, fresh
   thyme leaves
1 bay leaf
1/2 cup brandy
1/2 cup sherry
4 cups fish stock
1/4 cup tomato paste
1 1/2 cups heavy cream
1 1/2 tablespoons cornstarch
3 tablespoons water

In a 6-quart heavy kettle heat olive oil over medium high heat until hot but not smoking. Sauté lobster shells and body, stirring occasionally, 8 minutes. Add onion, celery, carrot, tomato, garlic, tarragon, thyme, bay leaf, brandy and sherry and simmer, stirring, until almost all liquid is evaporated, about 5 minutes. Add fish stock, reserved tomalley and the reserved cooking liquid. Simmer mixture, uncovered, stirring occasionally for 1 hour. Pour mixture through a fine sieve into a large saucepan, pressing on the solids until all liquid is through, then discarding the solids. Whisk in tomato paste and simmer until reduced to 3 cups, about 10 minutes. Add cream and simmer 5 minutes. In a small bowl stir together cornstarch and water and whisk into the bisque. Simmer, stirring, 2 minutes. Bisque will thicken slightly. Add lobster meat with any reserved juices and simmer 1 minute or until lobster meat is warm.

Makes 6 to 8 servings.

ROASTED CORN CHOWDER WITH JALAPENO-SCALLION OIL
Steve Cole

Jalapeno-Scallion Oil
3 scallions, cut into 2-inch pieces
1/2 fresh jalapeno pepper,
   including seeds
1/4 teaspoon kosher salt
1 cup canola oil

Chowder
1/2 pound smoked bacon, diced
2 tablespoons butter
1 large onion, chopped
1 cup minced celery
1 teaspoon minced garlic
1 1/2 pounds red potatoes, peeled
   and cut into 1/2-inch pieces
1 quart chicken stock or water
3 cups fresh corn, half may be
   skillet roasted
2 cups milk
1 1/2 cups cream
1 teaspoon fresh thyme
Freshly ground black pepper
   to taste
Kosher salt to taste
Italian parsley, minced, for garnish

For the jalapeno-scallion oil, in a blender container combine scallions, jalapeno, salt and canola oil and purée on high speed until smooth. Do not over blend, as mixture will darken if heat builds. Set aside for at least an hour. Makes 1 cup.

For the chowder, in a large, heavy pan cook the bacon slowly until fairly crisp. Remove bacon leaving half of the bacon grease. Add butter, onion, celery and garlic and sauté until tender; do not let mixture brown. Add potatoes and stock to onion mixture and bring to boil. Reduce heat and simmer, covered, for 10 minutes. Add bacon, corn, milk, cream, thyme and pepper to taste. Bring chowder to a low boil and simmer, uncovered, for 15 minutes, or until potatoes are tender. Add salt to taste. Garnish with Italian parsley and drizzle with jalapeno-scallion oil.

Makes 6 to 8 servings.

ROASTED LEEKS WITH PROSCIUTTO AND MOZZARELLA
Steve Cole

6 tablespoons butter

3 tablespoons olive oil

12 slender leeks, dark greens
    discarded, cleaned and trimmed

3 cups chicken stock

12 thin slices prosciutto

6 slices mozzarella cheese

Sea salt and freshly ground
    black pepper to taste

Tuscan olive oil

Preheat oven to 500 degrees. In a roasting pan combine butter and oil to coat bottom of pan. Arrange leeks in a single layer. Place in oven and roast for 12 minutes. Turn leeks over and roast another 5 minutes. Add stock, turn leeks over and roast for 10 minutes more. Remove from broth. Divide leeks into 4 "bundles" of 3 each. Wrap each bundle with 3 slices prosciutto. Place in ovenproof dish, top with cheese, and broil until cheese and prosciutto are crispy and bubbly. Season with sea salt and freshly ground black pepper. Drizzle with olive oil.

Makes 4 servings.

Nationally recognized restaurateur Steve Cole established the concept of fine dining to fight hunger in the Kansas City area when he launched a "Taste of the Nation" event in 1988. As chef and owner of Café Allegro, Steve was a leading influence on the local dining scene, and his tireless energy and enthusiasm were key in the formative years of this event.

CHEESY CORN BAKE
Fiorella's Jack Stack Barbecue

2 tablespoons butter
4 teaspoons all-purpose flour
1/8 teaspoon garlic powder
3/4 cup milk
6 ounces sharp cheddar cheese,
   shredded
3 ounces cream cheese, cubed
3 (10-ounce) packages frozen
   whole kernel corn, thawed
3 ounces ham, diced

Preheat oven to 350 degrees. Coat a 2-quart casserole dish with cooking spray. In a large saucepan over medium heat melt butter. Stir in flour and garlic powder. Add milk all at once. Cook, stirring constantly, over low heat until thickened. Add cheeses and continue cooking, stirring, until cheese is melted. Stir in corn and ham. Transfer mixture to casserole dish. Bake for 45 minutes.

Makes 10 to 12 servings.

YELLOW SQUASH AND SWEET ONION GRATIN
The Grille on Broadway

1/4 cup vegetable stock
1/4 cup cream cheese
1/4 cup tomato salsa
Cayenne pepper to taste
2 large yellow squash, sliced
1 large sweet onion, sliced
1/2 cup grated romano cheese

Preheat oven to 350 degrees. In a small saucepan over medium heat, combine vegetable stock, cream cheese, salsa and cayenne pepper and heat until cheese is melted. In a small baking dish, layer squash and onion. Pour the liquid mixture over and top with romano cheese. Bake for 30 minutes or until squash and onion are tender but not dry.

Makes 4 to 6 servings.

CHEF'S NOTE
Makes a unique side dish in place of potatoes or rice and is just as satisfying. Low in carbs, too!

FIELD GREENS AND APPLE SALAD
Union Cafe

Dressing
1/2 cup white vinegar
2 tablespoons apple cider vinegar
1/2 cup sugar
1/2 teaspoon salt
1 1/2 teaspoons dry mustard
2 tablespoons Worcestershire sauce
2 cups salad oil

Salad
6 to 8 cups field greens, washed
   and torn into bite-size pieces
2 Granny Smith apples, sliced
1/2 cup toasted pecans
1/2 cup crumbled blue cheese

For the dressing, in a food processor combine vinegars, sugar, salt, dry mustard and Worcestershire sauce until well blended. While processor is still running, add oil slowly to emulsify.

For the salad, in a large bowl combine greens, apples, pecans and blue cheese. Toss with dressing.

Makes 6 servings.

FENNEL AND BELGIAN ENDIVE SALAD
Steve Cole

4 medium fennel bulbs, cored,
   quartered and thinly sliced
1 1/2 cups freshly squeezed
   grapefruit juice
1 cup freshly squeezed
   orange juice
1/2 cup freshly squeezed
   lemon juice
1 tablespoon minced shallot
Pinch of kosher salt
Freshly ground black pepper
   to taste
1 teaspoon honey
1/2 cup extra virgin olive oil
6 heads Belgian endive,
   finely julienned
1/4 cup torn Italian parsley
24 parmesan curls, for garnish

In a glass bowl place the fennel and pour citrus juices over. Place in refrigerator and chill for 2 hours. Drain, reserving the juices in a small non-corrosive saucepan. Return the fennel to the refrigerator until ready to assemble salad. Over medium high heat, reduce the juices to 1/2 cup. Place in refrigerator until chilled. Using a food processor blend the shallot with the kosher salt, pepper and honey. Add the chilled juice. Slowly add the olive oil to create a light emulsion. In a large bowl, toss the fennel and endive with the vinaigrette. Add parsley and serve topped with parmesan curls.

Makes 12 servings.

HEIRLOOM TOMATO AND AVOCADO SALAD WITH LEMON HERB VINAIGRETTE

Joe D's Winebar Café and Patio

Vinaigrette

1 tablespoon roughly chopped
   fresh mint
1 tablespoon roughly chopped
   fresh oregano
1 tablespoon finely chopped shallots
1/4 cup extra virgin olive oil
3 tablespoons fresh lemon juice
Coarse sea salt and freshly
   ground black pepper to taste

Salad

1 1/2 pounds mixed heirloom
   tomatoes, some diced; others
   cut in half, quartered or sliced
8 green pimento-stuffed olives,
   sliced
1/2 small red onion, julienned
1 English cucumber, peeled and
   sliced 1/4-inch thick
1 avocado, peeled, pitted and
   sliced lengthwise
1 to 2 hearts of romaine lettuce,
   tear larger leaves, leave small
   ones whole
3 ounces queso fresco or feta
   cheese, crumbled

For the vinaigrette, in a small bowl combine mint, oregano, shallots, olive oil, lemon juice, salt and pepper. Whisk together and set aside.

For the salad, in a large bowl combine tomatoes, olives, onion and cucumber. Add a small amount of vinaigrette and toss lightly. Carefully fold in the avocado slices. Divide romaine lettuce among four plates, top with tomato-avocado mixture and crumble cheese over salad. Drizzle remaining vinaigrette over top of each. Serve immediately.

Makes 4 servings.

CHEF'S NOTE

A farmers' market is the best source for heirloom tomatoes. Select a variety of shapes and colors for the most interesting presentation.

GRILLED ASPARAGUS SALAD WITH ROASTED SHALLOT BALSAMIC VINAIGRETTE
Café Sebastienne

Balsamic Vinaigrette
1 cup extra virgin olive oil, divided
5 shallots, peeled
2 large cloves garlic, chopped
1/2 cup balsamic vinegar
1/4 cup honey
Salt and pepper to taste

Salad
1 pound asparagus, trimmed
2 to 3 tablespoons olive oil
1 1/2 cups diced pancetta
1 1/4 cups diced roasted potatoes
1 1/4 cups balsamic vinaigrette
2 poached eggs
Grated pecorino cheese,
   for garnish

For the dressing, preheat oven to 350 degrees. Brush baking sheet with 1/2 tablespoon olive oil. Place shallots on sheet and roast for 30 minutes. In a blender container combine the roasted shallots, garlic, vinegar, honey, salt and pepper. Purée, slowly adding remaining olive oil to emulsify. Makes 2 cups.

For the salad, brush asparagus with olive oil. Grill until tender, about 4 minutes. Arrange asparagus on 2 plates; set aside. In a medium skillet sauté pancetta until crispy. Drain, return pancetta to pan, and add potatoes and 1 1/4 cups vinaigrette, stirring to combine. Heat until just warm. Spoon over asparagus. Top each serving with a poached egg. Garnish with grated pecorino cheese.

Makes 2 servings.

CHEF'S NOTE
Try this dressing with other salads. For example, toss with a combination of 1/2 pound cooked baby green beans, 1 pint mixed baby tomatoes and 1/2 pound greens.

65

KIDS CAFE

After-school programs offer children a safe environment for play and development. Agencies that partner with Harvesters to offer Kids Cafe also get the opportunity to help combat childhood hunger. Kids Cafe complements the efforts of program partners by providing a free, wholesome evening meal and nutrition education to their existing program.

Kids in the Kitchen is the nutrition education and hands-on cooking program developed by the University of Missouri/Lincoln University Extension for use in Harvesters' Kids Cafes. The program teaches children the importance of good nutrition to their physical and mental development, while providing hands-on preparation of healthy meals and snacks.

It is much easier to start life with good nutrition habits than to change bad habits as adults.

...now for dessert

CHAMPAGNE ZABAGLIONE
Classic Cup

8 large egg yolks
1/2 cup sugar
Pinch salt
3/4 cup champagne
1 cup heavy whipping cream

In a stainless steel bowl whisk together the egg yolks, sugar and salt until pale and very thick. Whisk in the champagne. Fill a large bowl one-quarter full of ice water and set aside. In a large pot bring water to a boil. Place the bowl of egg mixture over the boiling water and whisk vigorously for about 5 minutes, until mixture is thick and tripled in volume. The zabaglione should mound when dropped from the whisk. Immediately put the bowl over the ice bath and whisk until cold. In another bowl whip the whipping cream until soft peaks form. Fold the cream into the zabaglione. Refrigerate until ready to serve.

Makes 5 cups.

CHEF'S NOTE
It has been said that zabaglione is one of Italy's great gifts to the rest of the world. Called "sabayon" in France, this ethereal delight can serve as a dessert by itself or as a sauce over berries, ice cream or cake.

CHOCOLATE CRÈME BRÛLÉE
MelBee's Bar & Restaurant

2 cups heavy cream

1/2 teaspoon ground cinnamon

1 cup sugar, divided

5 egg yolks, beaten

4 ounces semi-sweet chocolate,
   chopped

Preheat oven to 350 degrees. Coat 4 individual baking ramekins with cooking spray. In a saucepan bring cream, cinnamon and 1/2 cup of the sugar to a boil. Remove from heat. In a bowl mix together egg yolks and chocolate. Stir cream mixture into eggs a little at a time making sure not to cook the egg yolks. Whisk until all chocolate is melted. Place brûlée mixture in individual ramekins. Place ramekins in a baking dish and fill halfway up the sides with warm water. Bake for 30 to 45 minutes or until knife inserted in center comes out clean. Allow to cool, then place in refrigerator. When ready to serve, preheat the broiler. Sprinkle 1 tablespoon of sugar on top of each brûlée. Place the cups on a heavy baking sheet and broil for 2 minutes or until the tops have browned. Watch carefully, as the sugar can caramelize quickly. Serve immediately.

Makes 4 servings.

HONEY ALMOND CRÈME BRÛLÉE
City Tavern

4 cups heavy cream, divided
1/2 cup honey
8 egg yolks
1 cup sugar, divided
2 whole eggs

Preheat oven to 325 degrees. Heavily coat soufflé cups or other ovenproof glass containers with cooking spray. In a saucepan, warm 2 cups of the cream with honey. In a mixing bowl, mix the other 2 cups of cream with the eggs and 1/2 cup of the sugar. Temper egg mixture with honey mixture. Let sit until foam forms on top. Skim off foam and place in soufflé cups. Place cups in a baking pan and fill half way up the sides with tepid water. Bake for one hour or until knife inserted in center comes out clean. Allow to cool, then place in refrigerator. When ready to serve, preheat the broiler. Sprinkle 1 tablespoon of sugar on top of each brûlée. Place the cups on a heavy baking sheet and broil for 2 minutes or until the tops have browned. Watch carefully, as the sugar can caramelize quickly. Serve immediately.

Makes 8 servings.

TIRAMISU
Lidia Bastianich – Lidia's Kansas City

30 ladyfingers, divided
2 1/2 cups warm strong espresso
2 ounces semi-sweet chocolate,
   chopped, divided
Cocoa, for dusting
6 egg yolks
3/4 cup plus 1/3 cup sugar
1 1/4 pounds mascarpone cheese
2 cups heavy cream
1 1/2 tablespoons dark rum

CHEF'S NOTE

Americans have learned to love this delightful confection as a dessert. Italians, however, have long enjoyed it with a cup of espresso as a late afternoon snack...the translation of tiramisu from Italian is "pick me up."

Dip 18 of the ladyfingers in the espresso and use them to line the bottom of a 9 by 13-inch baking pan. Sprinkle half of the chocolate and a generous dusting of cocoa over the ladyfingers. Set aside. In a mixing bowl combine the egg yolks and 3/4 cup sugar and mix with an electric mixer on high, approximately 10 minutes. By hand, mix in the mascarpone until incorporated and relatively lump free. Set aside. In a mixing bowl whip the cream, the 1/3 cup sugar and the rum until stiff peaks are formed. Add the mascarpone mixture and whip again until thoroughly mixed. Spread half of the filling on top of the ladyfingers. Soak the remaining ladyfingers in the espresso and make a second layer, leaving space in between the ladyfingers. Sprinkle with the remaining chocolate and another dusting of the cocoa. Spread the remaining filling evenly over the ladyfingers and lightly sprinkle with cocoa. Cover and refrigerate for six hours or overnight. Before serving, sprinkle with a dusting of cocoa.

Makes 12 to 16 servings.

CITRUS MASCARPONE CANNOLI WITH RASPBERRY AND MANGO SAUCE

Steve Cole

20 cannoli shells
1/2 cup powdered sugar
Candied orange peel, for garnish
Mint leaves, for garnish

Raspberry Sauce
1 1/2 pints fresh raspberries
2 teaspoons water
3 tablespoons sugar
1 tablespoon lemon juice
2 teaspoons light rum

Mango Sauce
2 mangos, peeled
Juice of 2 oranges
Juice of 2 lemons
1/2 cup simple syrup

Mascarpone Filling
2 pounds mascarpone cheese
Zest from 4 each, oranges, limes and lemons, finely chopped
1/2 cup sugar
2 ounces triple sec

Wine Suggestion: Monchof Urziger Wurzgarten Auslese

For the raspberry sauce, in a saucepan combine the raspberries with water and bring to a boil, stirring occasionally. Add sugar, lemon juice and rum and stir to blend. Remove from heat. Using a food processor, purée until smooth. Strain through a fine sieve, cover and chill overnight.

For the mango sauce, in a saucepan combine all ingredients and bring to a boil. Remove from heat. Using a food processor, purée until smooth. Strain through a fine sieve, cover and chill overnight.

For the mascarpone filling, in a mixing bowl whip all ingredients together. Let sit 30 minutes to stiffen. To assemble, pipe the mascarpone mixture into the cannoli shells. Dust the shells lightly with powdered sugar. Place the raspberry sauce on half of each plate and the mango sauce on the other half. Place 2 cannoli on the center of each plate and garnish with candied orange peel and mint leaves.

Makes 10 servings.

CHOCOLATE ANGEL FOOD CAKE
Aixois

1 1/2 cups sugar, divided
3/4 cup all-purpose flour
1/4 cup cocoa powder
1/4 teaspoon salt
12 egg whites
1 1/2 teaspoons cream of tartar
1 1/2 teaspoons vanilla extract

Preheat oven to 350 degrees. Grease and flour an angel food cake pan. In a mixing bowl sift together 3/4 cup sugar, flour, cocoa and salt. In another mixing bowl beat the egg whites with the cream of tartar. When whites are frothy add remaining 3/4 cup sugar and the vanilla. Beat until it forms stiff peaks. Fold in the flour mixture. Mix just until combined. Pour into prepared pan. Bake for 40 minutes until the top springs back when lightly touched. Immediately invert cake, leaving in pan. Cool thoroughly. Loosen sides of cake from pan and remove.

Makes 12 servings.

CHOCOLATE ESPRESSO MOUSSE ROULADE
Rozelle Court Restaurant

Cake

4 ounces good quality semi-sweet
  chocolate
2 ounces good quality bittersweet
  chocolate
3 tablespoons water
2 tablespoons brandy
5 eggs, separated
3/4 cup powdered sugar, sifted
Pinch of salt

Filling

1 teaspoon instant espresso coffee
  powder or instant coffee
1 tablespoon boiling water
1 1/4 cups heavy cream
1 teaspoon sugar

Preheat oven to 350 degrees. Grease a 10 x 15-inch jellyroll pan and line with baking parchment.

For the cake, in a double boiler combine chocolates, water and brandy. Cook over medium-high heat, stirring until melted. Remove from heat and set aside to cool.

In a small bowl whisk the egg yolks with the sugar until pale in color. Fold in the melted chocolate mixture. Using an electric mixer whisk the egg whites with the salt to stiff peak stage. Fold a small amount of white mixture into the yolk mixture, to lighten the egg mixture, then gently fold in the remaining whites. Pour the mixture evenly into the prepared baking pan. Bake for 15 minutes. Remove from oven, and cool completely.

For the filling, dissolve the coffee in the water. In a mixing bowl whip the cream to soft peaks, and then fold in the coffee and sugar.

Turn the cake out onto a sheet of waxed or parchment paper dusted with powdered sugar. Peel off the parchment carefully by lifting the front corners and peeling it back toward you. Spread the filling evenly over the cake. Roll up the long side of the cake, jellyroll style, using the sugared paper to help. Discard the paper. Chill the roulade for several hours, seam side down before serving.

Makes 12 to 16 servings.

RASPBERRY CHEESECAKE LOLLIPOPS
Rozelle Court Restaurant

4 (8-ounce) packages cream
   cheese, at room temperature

1 1/4 cups sugar

2 tablespoons cornstarch

1 1/2 teaspoons vanilla extract

4 eggs

4 ounces sour cream

1/2 cup raspberry purée or
   seedless raspberry jam

30 chocolate "cigarette" or other
   cylinder-shaped cookies

16 ounces ice cream dipping
   chocolate, melted

Preheat oven to 300 degrees. Grease two 9-inch cake pans. Using an electric mixer cream the cream cheese until smooth. Add the sugar and mix well. Add the cornstarch and mix well, scraping the bottom of the bowl. Add the eggs, one at a time, mixing after each addition. Add the sour cream and raspberry purée and mix well. Pour into cake pans and bake 50 minutes until set and lightly golden on top. Cool completely. Line a baking sheet with parchment paper. Using a 1 1/2-inch to 2-inch scoop, scoop small balls and place on sheet pan. Stick a chocolate cigarette in each of the scoops and freeze until hard. Remove from freezer and dip each lollipop in melted chocolate up to the chocolate stick, drag against the side of the bowl to remove excess chocolate and place back on parchment-lined baking sheet. Return to the freezer until ready to serve.

Makes 30 Lollipops.

CHEF'S NOTE

Use these unique "lollipops" to garnish plates when serving the Chocolate Espresso Mousse Roulade (as was done at Forks & Corks in 2004) or serve alone as a sweet treat.

75

15-MINUTE MOLTEN CHOCOLATE MINI-CAKES
Grand Street Café

14 ounces semi-sweet chocolate,
    chopped
1 cup (2 sticks) unsalted butter
2 tablespoons strong coffee
1 cup sugar
4 eggs
1/2 cup flour

Preheat oven to 375 degrees. Spray 2 muffin pans with cooking spray. In a microwave safe bowl place chocolate, butter and coffee. Heat on high for 2 minutes, then stir. Continue to heat on high until melted. Watch carefully; do not overcook. Set aside to cool. In a large bowl whisk together sugar and eggs until well blended. Slowly add chocolate mixture to egg mixture, whisking until just blended. Fold in flour. Do not overmix. Pour into muffin tins, filling each 1/2 to 2/3 full and bake. Oven temperatures vary, so check the cakes after 15 minutes. If they're very moist on top, continue to bake and check again at two-minute intervals. Tops should be just puffed and slightly dry, but cakes will be "jiggly" and center will not be set. (Note: It is important that these cakes bake for the right amount of time. Too little and they'll be too runny, too much and they turn into cookies.) Cool briefly; cakes will fall slightly in center as they cool. Invert onto plates.

Makes 12 to 16 mini-cakes.

CHEF'S NOTE
Serve with whipped cream or ice cream.

If baking in a 9 by 13-inch pan, add 5 to 10 minutes to the baking time. Serve by spooning onto plates.

PUMPKIN GINGER POUND CAKE
Annedore's Fine Chocolates

1 cup (2 sticks) butter, at room
temperature

2 cups sugar

4 eggs

1 (15-ounce) can pumpkin

1 teaspoon vanilla

3 cups all-purpose flour

1/4 teaspoon salt

2 teaspoons baking powder

1 teaspoon baking soda

1 teaspoon cinnamon

1 teaspoon ground cloves

1 teaspoon ground ginger

1/2 cup diced crystallized ginger

Preheat oven to 350 degrees. Coat a bundt pan thoroughly with cooking spray. In a mixing bowl cream the butter and sugar until light and fluffy. Add eggs one at a time, mixing well. Add pumpkin and vanilla and mix well. In a large mixing bowl combine flour, salt, baking powder, baking soda, cinnamon, cloves, ginger and crystallized ginger. Add pumpkin mixture and mix well. Pour batter into bundt pan and bake for approximately 1 hour until toothpick inserted in the center comes out clean. Cool in pan 10 to 15 minutes then remove from pan and place on a rack to finish cooling.

Makes 12 servings.

FRESH APPLE CAKE
Salsman Catering and Event Planning

1 1/2 cups all-purpose flour, sifted
2 teaspoons baking soda
1 teaspoon cinnamon
1/4 teaspoon nutmeg
1 teaspoon salt
1/2 cup (1 stick) butter
1 1/2 cups sugar
2 eggs, well beaten
4 large apples, peeled and finely
   chopped (about 4 cups)
1 cup whole bran cereal

Preheat oven to 350 degrees. Grease a 9 by 13-inch baking pan. In a large bowl sift together flour, baking soda, cinnamon, nutmeg and salt. In a mixing bowl blend butter and sugar, beating until fluffy. Add eggs and beat well. Stir in apples, bran and flour mixture. Spread batter into pan. Bake for 40 minutes.

Makes 16 servings.

CHEF'S NOTE
Sprinkle with powdered sugar before serving.

RASPBERRY SCONES
Pierpont's at Union Station

2 cups plus 2 tablespoons flour, divided

1 tablespoon baking powder

1/2 teaspoon salt

1/2 cup plus 2 teaspoons sugar, divided

1/4 cup butter

1 cup heavy cream

1 egg, slightly beaten

2 cups raspberries

2 tablespoons melted butter

Preheat oven to 375 degrees. In a large bowl sift together 2 cups flour, baking powder, salt and 1/2 cup sugar. Mix well. Blend in 1/4 cup butter with forks or pastry blender until small crumbles appear. In a small bowl combine cream and egg, then add to the flour mixture and stir just to incorporate. Do not overmix. Place raspberries in a large bowl, sprinkle evenly with remaining 2 tablespoons flour, just to cover. Fold berries into batter. Mix gently to combine. Do not overmix. Turn out onto lightly floured surface and knead 4 to 5 times. Pat out to 3/4-inch thick. Cut into circles using a biscuit cutter and place on an ungreased cookie sheet. Drizzle top of each scone with melted butter and sprinkle with remaining sugar. Bake for 18 to 20 minutes, until golden brown on top. Remove from oven and cool slightly on rack before serving.

Makes 8 to 10 scones.

CHEF'S NOTE
Serve on top of any fruit cobbler or as a shortcake with berries in between layers of sliced scones.

TANGY LIME SHORTBREAD BARS
Arcadian Hall and Catering

Shortbread
2 cups all-purpose flour
1 cup (2 sticks) butter
1/2 cup sugar

Filling
6 eggs, beaten
2 cups sugar
3/4 cup lime juice
1 cup sweetened condensed milk
Few drops green food coloring

Powdered sugar, for topping

Preheat oven to 350 degrees. Spray a 9 by 13-inch baking pan with cooking spray. For the shortbread, in a food processor combine flour, butter and sugar and pulse quickly until clumps appear. Place mixture into baking pan and press down evenly. Bake for 20 minutes or until slightly browned. Cool completely.

For the filling, in a large bowl combine the eggs, sugar, lime juice and milk and whisk together. Add a few drops of food coloring until mixture turns a pale green color. Pour filling on top of shortbread and bake for 30 minutes more until set and knife inserted in center comes out clean. Refrigerate until completely cool before turning out and cutting into bars. When ready to serve sprinkle a little powdered sugar on top of bars, using a fine sieve.

Makes approximately 36 bars.

WHITE CHOCOLATE SHORTBREAD
Annedore's Fine Chocolates

3/4 cup (1 1/2 sticks) unsalted
   butter
1 3/4 cups all-purpose flour
1/2 teaspoon salt
3/4 cup powdered sugar
1/2 teaspoon vanilla
1 (6-ounce) package white
   chocolate chips

Preheat oven to 300 degrees. Grease an 8-inch square baking pan. In a mixing bowl using a pastry cutter, cut the butter into the flour and salt until mixture resembles cornmeal. Stir in the powdered sugar and drizzle in the vanilla. Knead in the white chocolate chips and press mixture into the baking pan. Bake for 40 to 50 minutes until golden brown. Cut while warm.

Makes 9 servings.

**Wine Suggestion:
Gould Campbell
1997 Late Bottled
Vintage Port**

GINGER SNAP COOKIES
Café Sebastienne

3 3/4 cups all-purpose flour

1 1/2 teaspoons baking powder

1/2 teaspoon baking soda

4 teaspoons ground ginger

1 1/2 teaspoons ground cinnamon

1/4 teaspoon ground cloves

1/4 teaspoon salt

3/4 cup (1 1/2 sticks) unsalted
   butter

1 2/3 cups sugar

2 large eggs

1/2 cup molasses

2 tablespoons fresh lemon juice

Zest of 2 lemons

Preheat oven to 350 degrees. Grease cookie sheets. In a large bowl combine flour, baking powder, baking soda, ginger, cinnamon, cloves and salt. Whisk to combine. In a mixing bowl cream butter and sugar until well blended. Add eggs, molasses, lemon juice and zest, beating until combined. Stir flour into molasses mixture until well blended and smooth. Form dough into 1-inch balls and place on cookie sheet. Flatten with a fork and bake 8 to 10 minutes.

Makes 3 dozen.

CHEF'S NOTE
Served at Chefs Classic with Lemon Ice Cream and Missouri Berry Compote (page 86).

APPLE COBBLER
Union Café

Filling

1/2 cup (1 stick) butter

8 cups peeled and thinly sliced
   tart cooking apples

1 3/4 cups brown sugar

1/2 teaspoon cinnamon

1/8 teaspoon allspice

1/4 cup orange juice

1 tablespoon orange zest

1 tablespoon balsamic vinegar

Streusel Topping

1 cup all-purpose flour

1 3/4 cups brown sugar

1 teaspoon cinnamon

1/2 teaspoon allspice

1/4 cup quick cooking or
   old-fashioned oats

1/2 cup (1 stick) butter, at room
   temperature

For the filling, melt butter in large pot. Add apples and stir to coat with butter. Reduce heat to medium, cover and cook for 5 to 7 minutes, until apples are soft on the outside, but still slightly crunchy. Add brown sugar, cinnamon, allspice, orange juice, orange zest and vinegar. Increase heat to high and cook at a rapid boil until juices become thick and syrupy, about 3 minutes. Remove from heat and allow to cool to room temperature.

For the topping, in a large bowl combine flour, sugar, cinnamon, allspice and oats. Fold in the butter and blend well until crumbly in texture.

Butter a 9 by 13-inch baking dish. Place filling in dish, and sprinkle topping over. Broil until golden brown.

Makes 12 servings.

**Wine Suggestion:
Palladino Moscato
d'Asti**

WALNUT-PEAR PAVÉ
Café Trocadero

Poached Pears

1 (750 ml) bottle burgundy wine

1 (750 ml) bottle tawny port

4 cinnamon sticks

4 cups sugar

1 1/3 cups brown sugar

12 red d'anjou or bartlett pears,
    peeled, cut in half, and cored

Syrup and Nut Filling

1 cup maple syrup

1/2 cup brown sugar

2 cups honey

1 teaspoon vanilla

1 teaspoon cinnamon

3 cups walnuts, toasted

Pastry

35 sheets frozen phyllo pastry,
    thawed

1 cup (2 sticks) unsalted butter,
    melted

For the pears, in a large saucepan combine the wine, port, cinnamon sticks, and sugars. Bring to a boil; reduce heat to medium low and add the pears, making sure they are covered with liquid. Simmer until pears are tender and rosy in color, about 25 minutes. Place pears, still covered in poaching liquid, in refrigerator until cool. Remove pears from liquid, slice lengthwise into 1/8-inch slices and set aside. Reserve 1 cup poaching liquid.

For the filling, in a medium saucepan combine syrup, brown sugar, honey, vanilla and cinnamon. Cook over high heat, stirring constantly until thickened, about 5 minutes. Remove from heat, add walnuts and mix until well coated. With a slotted spoon, remove walnuts and set aside to cool. Add reserved poaching liquid to syrup mixture, return to heat and cook over medium heat, about 5 to 10 minutes, or until bubbly. When nuts are cooled, chop them into pieces.

Preheat oven to 375 degrees. Butter a 9 by 13-inch baking pan. Lay a sheet of phyllo in the prepared pan and brush very lightly with melted butter; layer 4 more sheets, brushing each lightly with butter. Arrange a layer of sliced pears over dough. Repeat another 5 layers of dough, again brushing each sheet with butter, add a thin layer of walnuts and drizzle with syrup. Repeat the process with another 5 layers of dough, then a layer of pears, 5 layers of dough, walnuts and syrup, 5 layers of dough, ending with a layer of pears. Top with 10 sheets of dough. Bake for 35 to 45 minutes, until slightly browned. Remove from oven and place on rack to cool before cutting.

Makes 9 to 12 servings.

CHEF'S NOTE

Serve with vanilla bean or cinnamon ice cream.

For a unique taste, add a splash of well-aged balsamic vinegar.

Wine Suggestion: Campbell's Rutherglen Muscat

MISSOURI BERRY COMPOTE WITH LEMON ICE CREAM
Café Sebastienne

Missouri Berry Compote
3/4 cup sugar
1/2 cup water
1 cup stemmed strawberries
1 cup red raspberries
1 cup blueberries

Lemon Ice Cream
6 egg yolks
3/4 cup sugar
2 cups milk
Pinch salt
1 vanilla bean, split
1/2 cup lemon juice
Zest of two lemons

For the compote, in a saucepan over medium heat combine sugar and water and heat until hot. Add berries, reduce heat and let cook for 2 minutes. Cool slightly before serving. Makes 3 cups.

For the ice cream, in a medium saucepan over medium heat combine egg yolks, sugar, milk, salt and vanilla bean. Cook until mixture coats the back of a spoon. Add lemon juice and zest and stir to combine. Remove from heat. Chill overnight. Remove vanilla bean and freeze in an ice cream machine according to manufacturer's directions. Serve topped with Missouri Berry Compote.

Makes 3 cups compote.

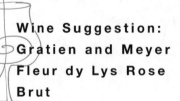

Wine Suggestion: Gratien and Meyer Fleur dy Lys Rose Brut

AMARETTO BREAD PUDDING
Arcadian Hall and Catering

Bread pudding

4 eggs

1 quart half and half

1 1/2 cups sugar

2 teaspoons almond extract

1 pound challah or egg rolls, cubed

3/4 cup golden raisins

3/4 cup sliced almonds

Amaretto sauce

1 cup powdered sugar

1/2 cup (1 stick) butter

1 egg, beaten

1/4 cup amaretto liqueur

Coat a 9 by 13-inch baking dish with cooking spray. In a large bowl whisk together eggs, half and half, sugar and almond extract. Fold in bread, raisins and almonds. Pour into baking dish. Cover with plastic wrap and refrigerate overnight. The bread will absorb the liquid. When ready to bake, remove pudding from refrigerator and allow to come to room temperature. Preheat oven to 325 degrees. Place pudding in the oven and bake for 45 minutes, until golden brown and firm and a knife inserted in the middle comes out clean.

For the amaretto sauce, in a saucepan combine all ingredients. Cook over low heat, stirring until butter is melted and mixture is smooth. Pour over the pudding and serve immediately.

Makes 8 servings.

TOASTED WALNUT FINANCIER
The American Restaurant

1 cup walnut flour

1/2 cup plus 1 tablespoon
   unsifted cake flour

2 3/4 cups sifted powdered sugar

5 large egg whites

1/2 cup chopped walnuts, toasted

2 sticks plus 4 tablespoons
   unsalted butter, melted and
   browned

Preheat oven to 375 degrees. Coat a financier mold (or other small molds) with cooking spray. In a mixing bowl combine walnut flour, cake flour, sugar, egg whites and walnuts. Using an electric mixer with a paddle attachment on low speed, mix until smooth. Slowly drizzle in the melted butter to emulsify. Pour into molds, filling each 3/4 full and bake for about 15 minutes or until golden brown.

Makes 6 to 8 servings.

CHEF'S NOTE
To make walnut flour, grind walnuts very finely in a food processor. Sift into a measuring cup. The ratio is two to one – 2 cups of halved walnuts yields 1 cup of walnut flour.

MAPLE ICE CREAM
The American Restaurant

1/4 cup dark amber 100-percent
   real maple syrup, no substitutions
3 cups cream
1 1/2 cups milk
1/2 teaspoon vanilla extract
1 1/4 cups sugar
8 egg yolks

In a saucepan over medium heat, combine the maple syrup, cream, milk and vanilla extract. Bring to a boil and remove from heat. In a mixing bowl combine the sugar and egg yolks, whisking until smooth. Slowly add the warm cream mixture to the egg mixture, stirring constantly. Return the mixture to the saucepan and gently warm the custard, stirring constantly with a heat resistant rubber spatula, until the mixture coats the back of a spoon. Be careful not to overcook the eggs. Strain through a fine mesh strainer and cool in an ice bath. Freeze in an ice cream machine according to manufacturer's directions. Serve with Walnut Financier.

Makes about 1 quart.

CHEF'S NOTE
Financier means "banker's style" in French. The name refers to the costly ingredients.

Thank You!

We gratefully acknowledge the support of the restaurants listed below...and in particular, the owners and chefs affiliated with these establishments. Without their assistance this cookbook would not have been possible. More importantly, without their ongoing support of Harvesters, thousands of Kansas Citians would go hungry each year. Thank you!

Aixois
American Restaurant, The
Annedore's Fine Chocolates
Arcadian Hall and Catering
Café Sebastienne
Café Trocadero
Capital Grille, The
Catering Company, The
City Tavern
Classic Cup
Doubletree

EBT Restaurant
Eddy's Catering
Feasts of Fancy Catering
Fiorella's Jack Stack Barbecue
40 Sardines
Frondizi's Ristorante
Grand Street Cafe
Grille on Broadway, The
Hannah Bistro Café
Hereford House
Isle of Capri - Farradays
Jazz - A Louisiana Kitchen
JJ's
Joe D's Winebar Café & Patio
K C Masterpiece Barbecue & Grill
La Bodega
Le Fou Frog
Lidia's Kansas City
McCormick and Schmick's
MelBee's Bar & Restaurant
Milano
Morton's, The Steakhouse – Kansas City
Paulo & Bill's
Pierpont's at Union Station
Piropos Restaurant
Remington's
Rozelle Court Restaurant
Salsman Catering and Event Planners
Savoy Grill
Tatsu's French Restaurant
Union Café

Thank You!

A collection such as this requires the efforts of so many! Thanks to the following for all the gathering, reviewing, revising, advising, encouraging, organizing, testing, tasting, writing, rewriting, proofreading, fact checking, coordinating and generally weaving together the myriad of details that make a book *happen*.

Karen Adler

Lidia Bastianich

Keith Baum,
   Premier Cru
   Wine Company

Michelle Brownlee

Steve Cole

Dennis Cross

Mary Ann Duckers

Judith Fertig

Jennifer Maloney

Kay Moffat

Kathy Moore

Patrick Quillec

Jeffrey Scott

Anne Simmons

Dan Swinney

Celina Tio

Mandy Waters

Roxanne Wyss

Willoughby Design Group

Walsworth Printing

Soups

...now for dessert

Cakes, Cookies and Baked Treats

Custards and Creamy Sweets

Index
of Recipes

Notes

Notes